THE POWER
TO BREAK FREE
WORKBOOK

For Victims & Survivors of Domestic Violence

By Anisha Durve, A.P.
Acupuncture Physician

Printed in the U.S.A.
Edited by Marielle Marne.
Cover and layout design by Anisha Durve.

ISBN- 978-9848923-1-0

The Power to Break Free: Surviving Domestic Violence
with a Special Reference to Abuse in Indian Marriages
& Companion Workbook for Victims & Survivors of Domestic Violence

Foreword by Kiran Bedi

THE POWER TO BREAK FREE

SURVIVING DOMESTIC VIOLENCE
With a Special Reference to Abuse in Indian Marriages

by Anisha Durve A.P.

Companion Guide to
The Power to Break Free: Surviving Domestic Violence

The Power To Break Free Workbook

For Victims & Survivors of Domestic Violence

By Anisha Durve, A.P.

**The psychology of abuse simplified.
The answers every victim has been looking for.
Groundbreaking information that has never yet
been presented in this field!**

Part 1 The Psychology of Abuse
- 5 sequential stages that systematically create an abuser
- 9 progressive steps for a woman to surrender her power and become conditioned to accept violence
- Signs of 6 types of abuse- physical, verbal, sexual, financial, religious, & social
- 5 stages in the newly revised cycle of violence
- Pyramid of power tactics
- Community's role in enabling abusers
- Vital role of therapists, advocates, medical caregivers, legal representatives, and law enforcement to assist in a victim's journey to break free

Part 2 My Fight for Freedom
- Author's own gripping personal story as a survivor of a 7 year abusive marriage

Part 3 Voices of Indian Women
- Dynamics of abuse within Indian Hindu community
- History of the DV movement within the larger South Asian community
- Riveting accounts of survivors in their journey to find freedom
- Overcoming the cultural taboo of divorce

This empowering book hopes to inspire all victims...freedom is around the corner. Every woman possesses the power to be free.

"The Power to Break Free is one of the most thorough and well-written explanations of intimate partner abuse that I have ever read. It is full of inspiration for abused women and guidance for those who assist them. A terrific addition to the domestic violence literature."

Lundy Bancroft, author of Should I Stay or Should I Go?

Available on www.Createspace.com or www.Amazon.com
List Price $22, 428 pgs & Workbook $11, 100 pgs

Proceeds are donated to the Power to Break Free Foundation dedicated to empowering women & ending domestic violence.

Please visit us at www.Power2BreakFree.com

See us on Youtube at http://www.youtube.com/watch?v=KSkAOXbge2M

Companion Guide

The Power to Break Free Workbook is for victims and survivors of domestic violence to facilitate healing, process the deep-seated trauma of abuse, and find the necessary steps to recovery. For victims currently still in an abusive relationship, these exercises will help to evaluate your relationship, the effect of the abuse, how safe you are, and provide clarity about your situation. Exercises to examine yourself, your partner, types of abuse, and power and control tactics will prove instrumental. How you can get help, enlist the aid of the community, deal with the difficulties of separation, and evaluate true change are mentioned here.

For survivors who have left their abusive partners, this workbook will build your strength and self-awareness and provide necessary tools to find closure. Healing exercises will increase your confidence in your ability to move forward and embrace a new abuse-free future. The last section contains inspirational quotes and space to write your reflections and insights. This is an excellent resource to use during healing retreats and workshops for victims.

The supportive material and exercises in this workbook are intended to be used in conjunction with reading the book The Power to Break Free: Surviving Domestic Violence, which explains the psychology of abuse in detail. Any victim or survivor of domestic violence will find this text answers many questions such as "How did this happen to me?" Please refer to the website www.Power2BreakFree.com for additional information and resources.

Mission Statement

To inspire, empower, and liberate women

escaping from gender violence

and fuel them with the awareness

that they possess the power to break free.

The Power to Break Free Foundation has a visionary approach
and strategy to address and eradicate gender violence.
It strives to provide education and outreach to established
domestic violence organizations and women's groups,
healing workshops and seminars for victims and survivors,
and focus on prevention for young girls worldwide.

Please visit our website at www.Power2BreakFree.com
for more information on how you can make a difference now.

ALL proceeds from this book are donated to supporting the work of this foundation.

BULK DISCOUNTS of both the book and companion workbook are available for gender violence
and Indian organizations. Please email powertobreakfree@gmail.com to inquire.

Table of Contents

Table of Contents

DEFINING A HEALTHY RELATIONSHIP

An abusive relationship inherently lacks the following essential traits that define a healthy relationship. These traits are derived from several domestic violence publications.[1] It is the recognition of these qualities that often makes you aware of what your relationship is painfully lacking. Checkmark which traits are lacking in your interaction with your partner and below each one describe why you grieve their absence.

☐ Trust, intimacy, empathy, patience, compassion

☐ Mutual support, encouragement, praise

☐ Share decision making and daily household responsibilities

☐ Freedom to express opinions, tolerance, willingness to listen to other viewpoints

☐ Personal feelings and experiences are validated and acknowledged as real

☐ Communication involving honesty, negotiation, compromise

☐ Respect individual values, beliefs, ideas, expression

☐ Pursue individual interests, hobbies, activities, goals, friendships

☐ Encourage relationships with family, friends, and social support network

☐ Healthy boundaries, respect individual space and privacy

☐ Physical contact is non-threatening, expresses love, safety, comfort, and assurance

☐ No verbal abuse, criticism, judgment, ridicule, or name-calling

☐ Receive an apology if hurt, you are not made a victim of his rage

MYTHS OF ABUSE

Unveiling the silence and secrecy surrounding domestic violence involves confronting the stereotypes of abuse perpetuated by the community. It is imperative to dispel these common myths with enhanced social awareness, rigorous education and outreach. How many of these myths did you use to believe prior to becoming a victim yourself?

- ☐ The number of women who undergo abuse is insignificant.
- ☐ If there is no physical violence, a relationship is not abusive.
- ☐ Sometimes it is justifiable for a husband to hit his wife.
- ☐ Unless a woman has physical injuries or requires medical care it is not abuse.
- ☐ Educated people are not abusive.
- ☐ Abuse only occurs in low-income families and does not affect the middle-class or wealthy.
- ☐ The wealthier a couple is, the less severe the abuse.
- ☐ Anyone involved in an abusive relationship must have grown up in an abusive family.
- ☐ Abuse is limited to those in heterosexual relationships.
- ☐ Cultural stereotypes and beliefs do not affect abusiveness.
- ☐ Battered women imagine, exaggerate, deliberately fabricate, or initiate the violence.[2]
- ☐ Battered women somehow provoke or are to blame for the violence.[3]
- ☐ If children do not directly witness the abuse, they are not affected by it.
- ☐ The abuser never targets the children or uses them to manipulate his partner.
- ☐ An abusive father is better than no father at all.[4]
- ☐ It is easy for an abusive relationship to change for the better.
- ☐ Domestic violence is about a loss of control and anger management issues.
- ☐ Abuse does not occur in certain minority groups.
- ☐ Abuse does not occur among immigrants.
- ☐ Love marriages are free of abuse. Abuse only occurs in culturally arranged marriages.
- ☐ Women are always to blame if their husbands are abusive.
- ☐ Abuse by in-laws only occurs when they are living in the same household.
- ☐ If the in-laws are abusive, the spouse will always intervene on his wife's behalf.
- ☐ If abusive in-laws are removed from the equation, the wife can lead an abuse-free life.

Which of these myths prevented you from recognizing your own victimization because you could not identify with them?

NEW WHEEL OF POWER

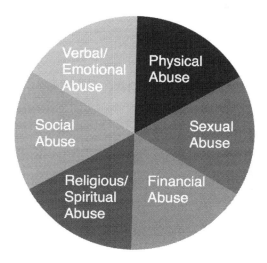

Definition of Abuse: Abuse can be defined as any systematic pattern of behavior employing various strategic tactics that use power and control to exert dominance over another being.

Which type of abuse was the most damaging for you? Why?

Describe the physical, mental, emotional, and spiritual effects of the abuse over the years.

PYRAMID OF POWER

Describe how your partner used each of these tactics to his advantage:

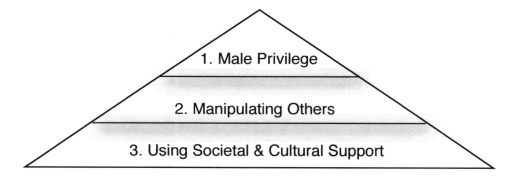

☐ **Male privilege** to establish his position as head of the household or "king of his castle."

☐ **Manipulating others** can implicate children, in-laws, family members, colleagues, or others.

☐ **Using society and culture** can include the religious community for example.

RELATIONSHIP BETWEEN ABUSER & VICTIM

Abusive relationship dynamic: Describe your experience with each of the 3 critical elements that characterize this dynamic.

(1) Constant dynamic of power and control

(2) Disrespect leading to a lack of real intimacy or empathy

(3) Unhealthy attachment often mistaken for love or affection

3 Major Behavior Patterns: The common myth that perpetuates abuse is the idea perpetrators are out of control, act unconsciously, and are unable to manage their tempers. Even though this is what he would like you to believe, this is simply not true. Describe your experience with each of these patterns:

(1) Unwillingness to resolve conflicts with you non-abusively

(2) Persistent choice to use violence against you

(3) Manipulative techniques

NEW CYCLE OF VIOLENCE

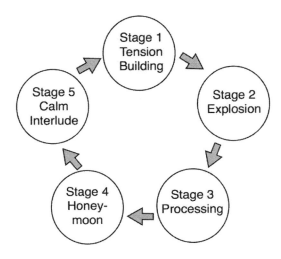

Describe your most challenging experience with each stage:

Stage 1 *Tension building stage:* pressure builds, warning signs manifest.

Stage 2 *Explosive stage:* unpreventable and destructive explosion, abusive incident.

*Stage 3 *Processing stage*: critical stage where you both come to terms with abusive incident differently, *not included in the original cycle of violence. Includes his denial and your acceptance.

Stage 4 *Honeymoon stage*: false hope and apologies, builds emotional attachment.

Stage 5 *Calm Interlude:* everyday "normal" life and routine resumes as if abusive incident never happened.

ESCALATION OF VIOLENCE

Checkmark whichever signs apply to your specific situation.

DANGER SIGNS of abuse escalating: Adapted from *Why Does He Do That?*[5]
- ❑ His behavior becomes increasingly suspicious, more threatening, or extreme.
- ❑ You begin to feel increasingly nervous around him but are not necessarily sure why.
- ❑ Your isolation is more noticeable as your contact with family and friends is increasingly restricted. He may claim you do not need anyone but each other.
- ❑ Acts like your rescuer and says you are no one without him.
- ❑ He reacts strongly to any steps you take to separate from him or end the relationship.
- ❑ His isolation builds and there is no one he is really close to.
- ❑ He becomes increasingly withdrawn, depressed, or suicidal.
- ❑ He becomes more obsessed with you and monitors your activities.
- ❑ He refuses to let you go to work.
- ❑ He starts to stalk you.
- ❑ He takes an interest in weapons or gains access to weapons.
- ❑ The violence starts to escalate in frequency or severity.
- ❑ He becomes violent during your pregnancy for the first time or the violence intensifies as he feels more threatened.
- ❑ He starts to abuse substances more heavily or uses them as an excuse for his hostile behavior.
- ❑ He obtains personal contact information or addresses for people you know: family, friends, workplace, school, etc. He threatens violence against other people.
- ❑ Resorts to threats, intimidation, and bullying.
- ❑ Becomes suspicious of others and believes they will convince you to leave him.
- ❑ He breaks or strikes things in anger. He uses symbolic violence (tearing a wedding photo, marring a face in a photo, etc.)
- ❑ His violence increases and your injuries require medical attention.

Identifying Specific Risk Factors:[6]
- ❑ Abuser is unemployed, has access to firearms, lives with you, your child by a previous partner lives in the home with him, he forces sex.
- ❑ You have left or are about to leave.
- ❑ Restraining order is about to be served.
- ❑ Abuser has been released from prison.
- ❑ Abuser has been notified of a recent separation, divorce, or custody change.
- ❑ He finds out you have reached out for help for the first time; his behavior has become "public."
- ❑ Abuser is currently using alcohol or drugs.
- ❑ You are showing signs of independence, have obtained a job or promotion, bought a car, or started school.

Guidelines to Disengage from his Power & Control Tactics:
- ❑ See how he actively tries to push your buttons. Identify your vulnerabilities he tries to exploit.
- ❑ Stay detached from the negative feelings and reactions he attempts to trigger in you.
- ❑ Distance yourself from his projections, blame, and accusations and do not personalize them.
- ❑ Resist being in a reactionary mode and do not try to retaliate or challenge him in any way.
- ❑ Identify his irrational behavior and do not attempt to rationalize with him.
- ❑ "Do not negotiate, no matter how much he wants to. This is not a discussion of how to improve things, correct things, change the past, find blame, or start over."[7]
- ❑ "Seek and apply strategies that make you unavailable to your pursuer."[8]

ACRONYMS FOR POWER & CONTROL

POWER: Describe how your partner manifested some of these behavior tactics.

Projection

Oppression

Will

Entitlement

Rage

CONTROL: Describe how your partner used some of these strategies for control when he was verbally abusive.

Criticize

Oppress

Neglect

Trivialize

Ridicule

Orde

Lie

VERBAL/ EMOTIONAL ABUSE

Checkmark any conversational control tactics your partner subjected you to.

☐ Abusive anger

Accuses

Belligerent

Belittles

Blames

Blocks- ends discussion

Brainwashes

Bullies

Chastises

Confuses

Contemptuous

Controls

Counters beliefs, ideas, actions

Criticizes excessively & harshly

Damages relations with others

Dehumanizes

Defensive

Denial

Denigrates

Discounts your beliefs

Disguises abuse as concern

Disparages your ideas

Diverts blame and accusation

Dominates

Exaggerates

Explodes verbally if irritated

Exploits

☐ Forgets abusive incidents

Glares, gives you "the look"

Harasses

Humiliates

Ignores you

Insults

Interrupts, refuses to listen

Intimidates

Invalidates you

Isolates you from others

Jealous comments

Jokes- sexist/offensive

Judges

Laughs at your opinions

Lies- speaks falsely of you

Manipulates

Mind Control/ plays mind games

Minimizes abuse

Misrepresents truth

Mocks

Nags

Name calling, put-downs

Neglects

Obsessive behavior

Oppressive

Orders and dictates

Patronizes

☐ Plays victim

Possessive

Pressures you

Provokes fear, guilt, obligation

Rage that is explosive

Rejects your opinions

Ridicules

Rolls his eyes

Sarcastic

Scorns, rebuffs

Scrutinizes

Silent treatment

Smirks

Sulks when upset

Swears, uses offensive language

Teases and jokes hurtfully

Temper tantrums

Threatens

Turns people against you

Trivializes your needs

Twists truth for his convenience

Undermines you

Unresponsive

Walks away

Withholds affection

Yells and shouts

Which verbally abusive behaviors affected you the most? Why?

PHYSICAL ABUSE

Checkmark any violent acts you have experienced.

❏ Beats	❏ Cuts	❏ Pinches	❏ Punches	❏ Slaps	❏ Strike
❏ Bites	❏ Grabs	❏ Pokes	❏ Pushes	❏ Stabs	❏ Throws objects at you
❏ Burns	❏ Hits	❏ Pounds	❏ Shakes	❏ Stomps	❏ Throws you around
❏ Chokes	❏ Kicks	❏ Pulls hair	❏ Shoves	❏ Strangles	❏ Wrestles

Intimidation Tactics:
❏ Blocks doorway or corners you in room so there is no escape
❏ Locks you in home so you cannot leave
❏ Locks you outside home so you have no access or way to get in
❏ Bullying response
❏ Cuts or tears your clothing, photographs, personal items
❏ Destroys your personal property, possessions, and anything that is meaningful to you
❏ Displays weapons to scare you
❏ Invades your personal space by getting too close so you feel uncomfortable
❏ Hits you when you are pregnant
❏ Kicks doors, windows, or objects
❏ Makes you flinch
❏ Points his finger in your face
❏ Punches wall or other objects to show his strength
❏ Raises his fist menacingly as if to hit you
❏ Stalks you so you have no privacy
❏ Threatens to hurt you, pets, children, family, or others
❏ Towers over you
❏ Walks toward you in an intimidating way
❏ Wildly gesticulates when he is angry and waves arms at you

Methods of Physical Restraint:
❏ Holds you down
❏ Pins you against the wall
❏ Places his body weight on top of you
❏ Prevents you from moving or leaving
❏ Restricts your freedom of movement
❏ Uses contact with your body to control or intimidate you
❏ Blocks you from using self defense

Which of these behaviors traumatized you the most. Why?

PHYSICAL INJURIES

Physical Injuries: Adapted from *The Battered Woman*[9]
- ❑ **Bleeding injuries**: wounds requiring stitches around face and head, facial wounds, bruises, swollen eyes and noses, lost teeth.
- ❑ **Internal injuries** cause bleeding and malfunctioning of organs such as damaged spleens, kidneys, or punctured lungs. Concussions, losing consciousness, surgeries, and blows to abdomen when pregnant.
- ❑ **Bones**: cracked vertebrae, skulls, and pelvises. Injured ribs, broken jaws, necks, backs, arms, legs, and collarbones.
- ❑ **Burns**: from cigarettes, hot appliances, stoves, irons, acid, or scalding liquids.
- ❑ **During pregnancy**- mutilated vaginas, sliced off nipples, repeated blows to protruding stomachs, miscarriage, stillbirth, infants born deformed as a result.
- ❑ **Sexual Injuries**- injuries to the genitals, lacerations, soreness, bruising, torn muscles, fatigue, vomiting, miscarriage, stillbirth, bladder infection, sexually transmitted diseases, and fistulas.[10]
- ❑ **Psychosomatic ailments:** backaches, headaches, stomach ailments, respiratory problems, eczema and other skin rashes, hypertension, other disorders caused by stress and anxiety.
- ❑ **More emotional** and less physical: anxiety attacks, palpitations, hyperventilation, severe crying spells.

Describe your most traumatic injury here. List any other physical injuries you experienced:

SEXUAL ABUSE

Checkmark tactics your abuser used to sexually control you and feel powerful.
- ❑ Rape
- ❑ Drug facilitated sexual assault
- ❑ Forcing you into sexually coercive or perverse acts
- ❑ Intentionally exposes you to sexually transmitted infections (STIs)
- ❑ Degrading you sexually
- ❑ Sexual harassment
- ❑ Promiscuity, flirting with other women
- ❑ Threats of infidelity
- ❑ Objectifies and depersonalizes you
- ❑ Controls access to contraceptive use
- ❑ Interferes with or "sabotages" birth control
- ❑ Forces you to have an abortion
- ❑ Forcibly impregnates you against your will
- ❑ Refuses to let you be part of decision-making about whether to terminate or continue a pregnancy

What was most devastating about this type of abuse?

RELIGIOUS / SPIRITUAL ABUSE   Adapted from *It's My Life Now*[11]

❑ Denies your religious beliefs
❑ Defiles or destroys religious books
❑ Discredits or trivializes your ideas, opinions, views, and values as unimportant, silly, or unrealistic
❑ Uses religion to intimidate you: "If you don't do as I say, you'll go to hell."
❑ Justifies his controlling behaviors by using religion
❑ Rejects your cultural or ethnic heritage
❑ Ridicules your religion or religious beliefs
❑ States his beliefs are the only "right" beliefs
❑ Prevents you from observing holy days and rituals
❑ Forbids you from visiting temple/church, attending religious services, or participating in sacred ceremonies
❑ Uses sacred texts to justify the abuse
❑ Undermines you by garnering support from religious authorities

What was most devastating about this type of abuse?

FINANCIAL/ECONOMIC ABUSE   Adapted from *Free Yourself From an Abusive Relationship*[12]

❑ Controls how, when, and where money is spent
❑ Restrictive allowance dictates amount you can spend
❑ Intensely critical of how you spend money
❑ Limits access or refuses to share income
❑ Cuts off access to credit cards or bank accounts
❑ Makes subtle or overt financial threats
❑ Restricts decision making abilities and spending rights
❑ Spends money freely on himself
❑ Withholds information about finances
❑ Purposely drains your assets to maintain control and ensure your dependence
❑ Takes economic advantage by forcing you to work and hoarding all the income
❑ Economically dependent on you to support the household
❑ Refuses to let you get a job or makes it difficult to keep your existing job
❑ Restricts access so all bank accounts are in his name only
❑ Limits access to basic resources or necessities
❑ Denies finances for medical bills so you do not get adequate health care
❑ He uses money to control your activities, purchases, and behavior[13]

What was most devastating about this type of abuse?

SIGNS DURING COURTSHIP

Victims must pay attention to these early signs an abuser might display when trying to win you over during courtship. Checkmark any of these signs that applied to your specific situation when you first met your spouse.

Attractive Qualities an Abuser May Display:

- ❑ Charming, exciting, captivating
- ❑ Playful, fun-loving, affectionate, kind
- ❑ Loving, attentive, warm, caring, devoted
- ❑ Sensitive, thoughtful
- ❑ Confidence, sense of ease, ability to take charge
- ❑ Magnetic personality, can mesmerize an audience
- ❑ Great sense of humor, entertaining
- ❑ Protective, acts concerned about your welfare
- ❑ Possessive, made you feel special, like you were the only one who matters
- ❑ Well respected in the community, successful, and held in high-esteem at work[14]
- ❑ Friends who look up to him and think the world of him[15]
- ❑ Close relationships to mother, sisters, or female friends[16]

Early Warning Signs of Abuser's Personality: Adapted from *Ditch That Jerk* [17]

- ❑ Verbally dominant
- ❑ Sense of entitlement
- ❑ Narcissistic personality
- ❑ Oversensitive to small slights
- ❑ Jealous or possessive
- ❑ Moody and unpredictable
- ❑ Critical, perfectionist, and tries to control everything
- ❑ Blames others for his problems and always plays the victim
- ❑ Victim mentality-believes the world is unfair and everyone is always out to get him
- ❑ Demands respect and is angry when he does not receive it
- ❑ Pressures you for sex
- ❑ Resists change, inflexible, unwilling to compromise.[18]

Warning Signs of Victim's Behavior: *Adapted from Why Is It Always About You?*[19]

- ❑ Lose yourself the more you get caught up in his fantasies and unreality.
- ❑ You choose to believe the image he projects and his potential, overlooking his shortcomings in the moment.
- ❑ You keep making excuses for his behavior.
- ❑ If he lies, cheats, disrespects, or hurts others, displays his lack of compassion, or betrays others' confidence, sooner or later, he will do the same to you.
- ❑ Do not feel assured you can change him or he will choose to change because of his feelings for you.
- ❑ If you cannot control your own need to idealize, you may be standing in the way of your own happiness.

ABUSER'S DECEPTION

Dual Personality: In each column below, list the traits that contrast between your partner's outer persona he displayed to others versus his private persona when he was alone with you.

Outer Persona	*Private Persona*

Betrayal: Write about the betrayal you feel from your partner's deceptive persona when courting you to recognizing his true abusive nature down the road. How long did it take you to see his duplicity? What red flags were there?

Benefits of Abusive Behavior: Abusers have a deep-seated resistance to change because they find their behavior benefits them in numerous ways. Checkmark any of the following behaviors that you believe served your partner. List adapted from *Why Does He Do That?*[20]

- ☐ Intrinsic satisfaction of power and control
- ☐ Getting his way
- ☐ Someone on whom to take out his problems
- ☐ Free labor from his spouse while he enjoys leisure and freedom
- ☐ Being center of attention with priority given to his needs and satisfying his ego
- ☐ Financial control
- ☐ Ensuring his career, education, and goals are prioritized
- ☐ Public status of partner/father without the sacrifices
- ☐ Approval of friends and relatives
- ☐ Ability to enforce double standards

MYTHS OF ABUSERS

The myths that conceal an abuser's true nature are oftentimes perpetuated and upheld by the aggressor himself to create confusion, portray himself as the victim, seek sympathy from others, and defend or justify his behavior. How many of these myths did you believe prior to becoming a victim yourself? Checkmark any myths that your abuser used as an excuse for his behavior.

- ❏ Loses control easily, quick to anger, uncontrollable temper
- ❏ Aggressive personality by nature
- ❏ Violent in all of his relationships
- ❏ Low self-esteem, trust and intimacy issues
- ❏ Internalizes feelings and has difficulty expressing them
- ❏ Poor communication skills
- ❏ Tremendous stress from his work environment, mistreated by boss or colleagues
- ❏ Masters of the hard luck story
- ❏ Difficult childhood filled with struggles
- ❏ Abused as a child
- ❏ Hurt by previous partners
- ❏ Afraid of intimacy and abandonment
- ❏ Only abusive to those he loves and cares for the most
- ❏ Hates women and does not have close relationships to the women in his life
- ❏ Substance abuser, may be addicted to alcohol or other drugs
- ❏ Mentally ill or personality disorder
- ❏ Victim of racism or prejudice
- ❏ Not religious minded or active in his religious community
- ❏ Assumed he cannot be well respected, a leader, or in a powerful position in society
- ❏ Can still be a good father to his children despite mistreatment of his wife
- ❏ Rarely targets children or uses them as pawns to manipulate his partner
- ❏ Pious devout men who are not abusive towards their wives.
- ❏ If living in a joint household with in-laws, husbands will always treat their wives well.
- ❏ A husband will always step in if others mistreat his wife.

Which of these myths infuriates you the most? Why?

CREATION OF AN ABUSER

The 5 steps and 11 layers that shape and create an abusive personality are summarized below. On the following page write next to each box which of these layers you believe most influenced your partner in creating his destructive personality.

STEP 1 **Exposure** to violence or destructive tendencies creates a memorable impression whether it is through:
Layer 1 Family Background
    a. Observe dynamics of unhealthy relationship between parents
    b. Witness father or role model being abusive and learns to imitate him
    c. Possibly victimized or abused himself which leads to feeling powerless
    d. Lack of quality psychological nurturing by parents who may be unreliable, unstable, unpredictable, absent emotionally or physically, or excessively critical
Layer 2 Role of Socialization
    a. Being bullied, teased, and dominated by others
    b. Socially isolated and ostracized by peers, interact superficially, and usually become loners
    c. Self-esteem diminished and feels socially inadequate
Layer 3 Societal/ Cultural Influences
    a. Patriarchal society emphasizes the subordinate status of women
    b. Religious hierarchy may highlight male dominance and beliefs in sexism
    c. Cultural or ethnic beliefs in male privilege or bias of traditional gender stereotypes
    d. Media glorifies violence and portrays women as sex objects

STEP 2 **Values:** internal mental environment and core elements of abusive mentality shaped
Layer 4 Abusive Attitudes
    a. Learns disrespect for women and lack of empathy
    b. Adopts oppressive mentality and distorted thinking
Layer 5 Sense of Entitlement
    a. Inflated ego can result from being raised with overindulgent praise and "excessive admiration that is never balanced with realistic feedback."[21] A child becomes dependent on excelling in his parents' eyes when he feels their love is contingent on his performance or achievements. Many Indian boys are raised with this sense of entitlement.
    b. Develops superiority complex and believes he is always right, so by default, his spouse must be wrong. His rigid thought pattern makes him intolerant of any opposition or conflicting view.

STEP 3 **Injury:** internalizes and represses internal conflict as a young child
Layer 6 Distorted Self-image
    Distorted self-image can result from feeling unimportant, unloved, and unvalued
Layer 7 Narcissistic Injury
    Must find a way to respond to threat of narcissistic injury

STEP 4 **Builds Defenses** to fiercely protect his wounded fragile self to avoid being hurt again.
Layer 8 Self-worth
Becomes deeply dependent of others' views to shape his self-worth.
    a. Consumed by deep-seated need for acceptance, approval, recognition, and constant validation, whether his ego is inflated or deflated.
    b. Seeks praise, prestige, and power to compensate for his sense of powerlessness, insecurity, and unworthiness.
Layer 9 Dominant Personality
Creates a dominant controlling personality to portray a confident image.
    a. Works overtime to compensate for his defect and prove himself.
    b. Adopts strategies such as a deceptively charming personality to serve as a decoy.

CREATION OF AN ABUSER

***STEP 5* Enabled**

Layer 10 Benefits Experience benefits from abusive relationship
   a. Learn that abusiveness is rewarding and makes him feel powerful
   b. Destructive pattern reinforced with time and each successive relationship
   c. Learns how to justify his behavior, make excuses, and deny its destructive effects

Layer 11 Enabled Community inadvertently enables perpetrator
   a. Learns he can get away with being abusive and not be held accountable for his actions
   b. Family, friends, peers, or society appear "tolerant" of abusive behaviors when they do not take a definitive stand or speak out against him
   c. Religious leaders/community may condone his actions
   d. His therapist may validate him so he feels supported
   e. Legal system and law enforcement may enable or protect the abuser's rights

STEP 1 EXPOSURE
Family Background
Socialization
Societal & Cultural Influences

STEP 2 VALUES
Abusive Attitudes
Entitlement

STEP 3 INJURY
Personal Inadequacy
Distorted Self-Esteem

STEP 4 DEFENSE
Seeks Praise, Prestige, and Power
Creates Dominant Personality

STEP 5 ENABLED
Experience Benefits of Abusiveness
Feels Supported by Community

3 TYPES OF ABUSERS

Checkmark as many traits from each of the three personality groups that applies to your partner. (Adapted from series of personality types in *Why Does He Do That?*)

The Player [22]

- ☐ Maintains a tough macho exterior and views women as delicate, inferior, in need of protection, and to be kept in line
- ☐ Flirtatious, jealous, possessive, and disrespectful towards women
- ☐ You feel violated, debased, used, or treated like a sex object
- ☐ Selfish, callous towards your feelings, and inattentive to your desires
- ☐ Dishonest, irresponsible, or engages in risky behavior

Dominating/ Mr. Right [23]

- ☐ Entitled, arrogant, condescending, and believes he is the ultimate authority on everything
- ☐ Highly distorted self-image leads him to believe he is above criticism and reproach, has no faults, and cannot be challenged
- ☐ Intolerant of others' opinions and is personally offended if you disagree with him
- ☐ Dominates conversations with his opinionated views, thrives on debating
- ☐ Harps on your faults and offers relentless advice on every aspect of your life
- ☐ Demanding, threatening, intimidating, aggressive, and manipulative
- ☐ General attitude is that you exist to serve all his needs and should feel grateful and lucky to be with him.

The Victim/ Mr. Sensitive [24]

- ☐ Always plays the victim
- ☐ Claims he is constantly misunderstood, bullied by everyone, and truly believes he is never at fault
- ☐ Complains life in general is unfair
- ☐ Feels underestimated
- ☐ Blames you and everyone else for his problems
- ☐ Appeals to your compassion and constantly focuses on his hurt feelings to avoid discussing yours
- ☐ Not necessarily outwardly aggressive, may act calm, be soft-spoken, and never raise his voice
- ☐ Subtle tactics include a steady stream of emotional assaults that may be difficult to identify

Which type of abuser category or combination of categories best describes your partner?

MYTHS OF VICTIMS

The following common myths contribute to the classic image or media-generated portrait of a battered woman. Seen as a "damsel in distress," victims are portrayed as defenseless, helpless on their own, and in need of rescuing. Your inability to identify with these stereotypes that may be vastly inconsistent with your own self-image is one of the greatest barriers to recognizing your victimization and inadvertently perpetuates abuse. Checkmark any of these myths that others believed were true about you.

- ❒ Low self-esteem, lack confidence, no self-worth
- ❒ Underprivileged, from low socio-economic class
- ❒ Not well educated or very intelligent, lack college degree or higher education
- ❒ Weak, timid, vulnerable, powerless
- ❒ Naïve, innocent, gullible, easy to take advantage of, too trusting of others
- ❒ Tolerant of violent behavior, conditioned to accept violence
- ❒ Grew up in violent households
- ❒ Abused as a child by father or dominant, influential male
- ❒ Feel the need to be protected by a man
- ❒ Drawn to domineering macho men, pattern of attracting abusive men into life
- ❒ Hurt by previous partners
- ❒ Prefer to be with abusive man instead of being single
- ❒ Enjoy being dominated and controlled by a man
- ❒ Believe you deserve to be abused
- ❒ "Would have left already if you did not like it"
- ❒ Wish to serve her husband and wait on him hand and foot
- ❒ Believe your place is in the home, taking care of the children, and not working
- ❒ Fit a cultural stereotype or image of being passive, docile, submissive
- ❒ Accept husband should make all decisions about home, finances, career, etc.
- ❒ If you are well educated, independent, and career minded, there is no way you can become susceptible to abuse

Which of these myths infuriates you the most? Why?

FEMALE STEREOTYPES

Checkmark any of the following stereotypes that you felt pressure to conform to and explain why. Did you feel pressure by society, your culture, your family, your religious beliefs, or yourself?

❐   Obedient, dedicated, patient

❐   Humble, chaste, pure, loyal

❐   Adjusting, supportive, nurturing

❐   Tolerant of husband's beliefs and behavior

❐   Docile demeanor, conforming, submissive to husband's will

❐   Sacrifice individual needs in the spirit of service and surrender

❐   Prioritize family unity

❐   Place the needs of children, husband, and in-laws first

❐   Endure hardship without complaining

❐   Restrain emotions and feelings

❐   Maintain all aspects of the household

❐   Bear responsibility for upholding family life and cultural traditions

4 PARTS TO FEMALE IDENTITY

Write how the abuse affected each of these aspects of your identity. How did you lose yourself in this process?

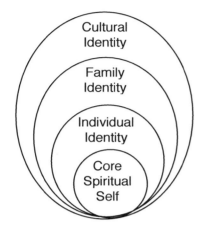

Broader cultural identity: How did you assimilate with the ideal stereotypes of your culture? Did these ideals emphasize submission, sacrifice, and surrender?

Family identity: How did you define yourself by your relationships to your husband and children?

Individual identity: How did you neglect prioritizing this and not give it much expression?

Core spiritual self: How did you repress this part of yourself?

9 STEPS TO BECOMING A VICTIM

The 9 steps a victim goes through to surrender her power are listed below. Steps 1 and 2 are the precursors that build up to abuse while steps 3-9 occur as you experience the stages in the cycle of violence. Answer the questions below to explore what you experienced during each step.

Step 1: Courtship-fall for abuser's charm and deception, believe in fairytale romance
Step 2: Ignore red flags-growing feeling of uneasiness and doubt, stop trusting your instincts
Step 3: Acceptance-response to first incident of abuse sets the pattern
Step 4: Increasing isolation
Step 5: Give up your voice-choose silence and secrecy
Step 6: Trapped-conflict of two opposing realities, cannot make sense of it, confusion builds
Step 7: Shift priorities-place him and his needs before yours as he conditions you to do
Step 8: Traumatic bonding-develop unhealthy attachment and loyalty
Step 9: Develop coping strategies for safety and survival

1) List his attractive qualities he used to deceptively win you over during the courtship.

2) List all the red flags you ignored. Why did you?

3) Describe the first incident of abuse. What was your first response?

4) How did he isolate you?

9 STEPS TO BECOMING A VICTIM

5) Why did you keep this a secret?

6) What are the two conflicting realities you experienced?

7) How did you prioritize him and neglect yourself?

8) In what ways were you attached?

9) List some of the ways you coped with the abuse.

5 COMMON TRAITS OF VICTIMS

Checkmark any of the following 5 attributes that characterize many victims if they describe you. There is nothing inherently wrong with any of these qualities but in an abusive environment they may have contributed to your victimization. Describe how it might have made you more susceptible to the abuse.

☐ *Traditionalist*-about home, family values, and female stereotypes to some extent. Strongly believe in preserving family unit at all cost and upholding the institution of marriage. This is reinforced by the abuser's similar belief system.

☐ *Idealistic*-view marriage as an ideal to be attained and to strive for. May focus on his positive attributes to the point of idealizing him and glossing over any negative traits.

☐ *Vulnerability*-marked by being at a place of transition or uncertainty in life. You are influenced by predisposing factors such as loneliness, heartbreak from prior romance, homesickness, moving, life change, financial worries, job insecurity or loss, career changes, completing school, loss of a loved one, and naïveté about violence. There is a yearning desire to feel safe, secure, protected, and find a mate who provides this sense of belonging.[25]

☐ *Compassionate nature*-tendency to be kind, patient, loving, and give him the benefit of the doubt. Believe a nurturing disposition will change him but are unaware of how he takes advantage of your generosity at first.

☐ *Power imbalance*-may admire and look up to your spouse's status, wealth, position, or education, and feel dependent on him for reassurance and support. There is a belief he will help improve your self-esteem, financial status, or social status.

4 LAYERS OF EMOTIONAL WOUNDING

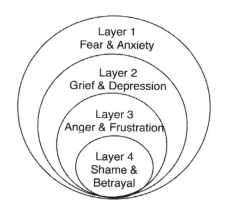

There are four layers of emotional wounding a victim can experience. For each layer describe your most intense emotions and how they affected you. How can you begin to heal this emotion?

Fear and anxiety:

Grief and depression:

Anger and frustration:

Shame and betrayal:

EFFECTS OF ABUSE & PTSD

Mental & Physical Wounding

In addition to the emotional wounding are the mental and physical effects of abuse that compound a woman's victimization. This response has four components:

- ☐ Shock
- ☐ Exhaustion
- ☐ Stress and hormonal imbalance
- ☐ Physical symptoms

Describe how your shock paralyzed you:

Describe how your exhaustion limited you:

Symptoms of Post-Traumatic Stress Disorder include severe stress reactions and psycho-physiological complaints, partially derived from *The Merck Manual*. Checkmark all that apply to you.

☐ **Anxiety**	Restlessness, fatigue, poor concentration, irritability, muscle tension, disturbed sleep, uncertainty, growing self-doubt, loss of self-confidence, palpitations.
☐ **Depression**	Withdrawn, not as involved in daily activities, lack enthusiasm, may be suicidal, flat affect or not talkative, trouble sleeping, poor appetite, can't experience other emotions, poor concentration, indecisive, helpless, hopeless, loss of sexual desire.
☐ **Fear**	Intense terror, intimidation, or sense of being helpless. Anticipation can be terrifying, fearful of future events or relationships.
☐ **Disturbed sleep**	Insomnia, restless sleep, difficulty falling or staying asleep, recurring distressing dreams, or nightmares.
☐ **Hyper-vigilance**	Easily startled, heightened startle reflex, learns to be on-guard, defensive, distrusts spontaneity.
☐ **Flashbacks**	Reliving thoughts and images of abuse suddenly without warning.
☐ **Numbness**	Detachment, lack of emotional responsiveness, inability to feel.
☐ **Avoidance**	Avoids abuse triggers or any stimuli associated with trauma, ominous feeling, intensely negative response to any abuse reminders, avoid talking about event, avoid people, places, or behaviors that might lead to distressing memories, inability to recall major parts of trauma. Desire to escape or run away, desire to not be "too sensitive," hesitancy to accept her perceptions, reluctance to come to conclusions.

EFFECTS & SYMPTOMS OF ABUSE

Panic attacks include the sudden appearance of at least 4 physiologic symptoms according to *The Merck Manual*:[26] Checkmark any symptoms you have experienced.

- ☐ Shortness of breath
- ☐ Palpitations or accelerated heart rate
- ☐ Chest pain or discomfort
- ☐ Profuse sweating
- ☐ Chills or feeling flushed
- ☐ Choking
- ☐ Dizziness
- ☐ Trembling or shaking
- ☐ Nausea, stomachache or diarrhea
- ☐ Numbness or tingling sensations
- ☐ Sense of "unreality" or detachment from environment
- ☐ Fear of dying or going crazy or losing control

Suicidal behavior includes the following self-destructive behaviors according to *The Merck Manual*:[27]

- ☐ Excessive drinking or drug use
- ☐ Heavy smoking
- ☐ Overeating
- ☐ Neglect of (your) health
- ☐ Self-mutilation
- ☐ Reckless driving
- ☐ Criminal behavior

What has been the most devastating mental or physical effect from the abuse? How have you worked towards healing from the trauma?

Breaking Point: *"The decisive turning points and precipitating events that emerged fell into one of the following categories:"*[28]

- ☐ His threats become increasingly severe.
- ☐ His public episodes of abuse are heightened.
- ☐ His violence increases and your injuries require medical attention.
- ☐ Your support network grows and you feel more confident about taking action.
- ☐ Your reasons for staying have been satisfied such as the birth of the youngest child or kids have graduated and gone to college.
- ☐ An extramarital affair reminds you you are desirable and not all men are abusive.

Describe your breaking point(s). What was your "final straw?" Was it one incident or multiple triggers?

6 COPING STRATEGIES

Next to each of the 6 primary strategies you probably utilized to cope with your abusive situation, give examples of what strategies you relied on and how it may have perpetuated the abuse.

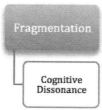

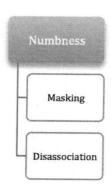

6 COPING STRATEGIES

Refer to *The Power to Break Free: Surviving Domestic Violence* for detailed descriptions of each of these categories.

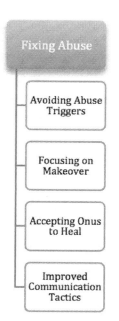

OBSTACLES TO RECOGNIZING ABUSE

There are numerous reasons why it is challenging for a woman to process she is a victim. Checkmark any of the following reasons why you hesitated to label your experience as abuse.

- ☐ **Insidiousness**: The nature of abuse is subtle. By constantly invalidating your perception of reality, he makes it challenging to see through his manipulation and deception.

- ☐ **Secrecy:** A perpetrator conceals his motivations and disguises his behavior well while possibly maintaining the outward appearance of a supportive, doting husband.

- ☐ **Blame:** You may accept partial blame when your spouse tactically turns your attention towards self-improvement instead of analyzing his behavior.

- ☐ **Denial:** It is inevitable you mimic your partner's denial when he constantly avoids admitting to the abuse and you start to doubt your sanity.

- ☐ **Conditioning:** With time, you adapt to the intensity of the abuse, accept the escalation of violence, and minimize or deny events.

- ☐ **History:** Never having witnessed violence, you may lack perspective to identify behavior that is so foreign to you. Or, if you do come from a background of abuse, this further complicates the situation, impairing your ability to distinguish unhealthy relationships as undesirable.

- ☐ **Media:** Biased by extreme horrific images of domestic violence, you may not relate unless you have severe brutal injuries or are forced to visit the emergency room.

- ☐ **Hope:** The eternal undying hope that your situation will improve with time characterizes all victims. You believe your partner's convincing promises he will change because he persistently and persuasively affirms this and have faith your marriage will work in the end.

Abuser's Excuses: Checkmark any of the typical excuses your partner may have used for his behavior.
- ☐ Stress from wedding and being a newlywed
- ☐ Anxiety, depression, or other emotional issues
- ☐ Low self-esteem
- ☐ Poor communication, misinterpretation
- ☐ Geographic moves
- ☐ Family pressure
- ☐ Job or career uncertainties
- ☐ Difficulty at work, pressure from boss, or job loss
- ☐ Blames the past or present
- ☐ Has to resort to violence to "protect" you
- ☐ Loses control and claims you are at fault for triggering him. Believes you are responsible for preventing an outburst by not upsetting him.
- ☐ Displeased when you irritate him and do not fulfill your "duties"
- ☐ Dealing with your first pregnancy and nervousness about being a father
- ☐ Substance abuse, blames his addiction for his mistreatment

List any other excuses your partner used to justify his behavior:

TRAPPED BY BELIEF SYSTEM

Ultimately, a victim is ensnared by her belief system, held prisoner by her own mind. This can come as a shock after feeling trapped by your spouse for so long. It takes time to process this shift in perspective. There are several factors in your thinking that may perpetuate abuse. Checkmark any of these beliefs that kept you trapped and below each write why you believed that.

❏   You believe your partner is rational and thus you rationalized the abuse and his behavior.

❏   You took responsibility for "fixing" the problem that you incorrectly diagnosed.

❏   You are fueled by your desire to have a "successful" marriage.

❏   You blame yourself for the "failure" of your marriage.

❏   Your undying hope that things will improve and change for the better makes you the eternal optimist.

REASONS FOR SILENCE & SECRECY

Checkmark all the reasons that apply to your specific situation. Below each one write why you chose to maintain your silence.

❒   Believe your predicament is unique and no one else will understand.

❒   Feel ashamed, embarrassed, and humiliated as you experience the loss of your dignity.

❒   Blame yourself for the abuse because he has conditioned you to do so.

❒   Unable to articulate your victimization because it is too painful to share the details with friends or family. You reason it is easier to keep silent.

❒   Fear rejection if no one believes you, especially if they are enamored with abuser and constantly tell you how lucky you are to be with him.

❒   Seek to preserve and protect your marriage and keep personal life intact.

❒   Feel ashamed to be perceived as a failure who could not make your marriage work.

❒   Fear abuser's repercussions of betraying him if he discovers you have spoken about abuse to others.

Are there any other reasons you maintained your silence?

Who have you kept your secret from that you wish you could confide in?

MYTHS ABOUT SEPARATION

Myths about Separation: Adapted from *It's My Life Now*.[29] Checkmark which myths you have heard from others when discussing your situation that may have re-traumatized you.

- ❑ If you do not leave an abusive relationship right away, there must be something wrong with you.
- ❑ Anyone who could love an abusive partner must be weak, insecure, and have other psychological issues.
- ❑ Once abused by your partner, all your love for him vanishes.
- ❑ There is no way for you to increase your safety if you continue to live with your spouse or if you separate from him.
- ❑ If there was no physical violence while you were in the relationship, there will not be any after you leave.
- ❑ Once survivors leave their abusive relationships, they would never consider returning to their abusers.
- ❑ Any survivor who returns to an abusive partner is weak and any further abuse is your fault.
- ❑ Survivors of domestic violence are victims who just can't make it on their own.
- ❑ Once you are out of the relationship, you are out of danger.
- ❑ The emotional turmoil you experience in the aftermath of an abusive relationship is brief and usually fairly mild.
- ❑ After leaving, you are free from any interactions with your partner. He can no longer exert control over you and will leave you alone.
- ❑ Dealing with the loss of an abusive relationship is easy, you feel a sense of relief, move on quickly, and your life becomes easier.
- ❑ You are doomed to repeat the cycle and are never again able to find a truly intimate loving relationship.
- ❑ Survivors become experts in predicting whether your next potential partner has controlling or violent tendencies.

Culturally Specific Myths:

- ❑ Regardless of whether you have a green card, immigrants are free to leave their abusive spouses at any time.
- ❑ Victims always have the opportunity to return to their natal homes and be welcomed by their families when separating from abusive husbands.
- ❑ Divorce is not a stigma in many minority cultures and an option you will readily consider as a viable solution to end abuse.
- ❑ Divorce is encouraged whenever abuse is disclosed.
- ❑ Returning home as a separated or divorced woman is acceptable in all families.
- ❑ Remarriage is equally as easy or viable as it is for men.

Which of these myths infuriates you the most? Why?

23 REASONS TO "STAY"

Victims choose to "stay" for numerous reasons. If any of these reasons applied to your specific situation, list how below.

(1) **Resist Change:** It is normal to gravitate to what is familiar, even if it means staying in an unhealthy situation. Any change is scary if you have been trapped in this pattern for years.

(2) **Safety:** Genuine fear for the personal safety of your children or yourself if you attempt to leave is valid and appropriate. Statistically, separation increases your risk of violence.

(3) **Threats:** The prospect of facing his threats, imagining his retaliation, and dealing with his unpredictability is daunting.

(4) **Paralyzed:** The sheer multitude of conflicting emotions you must process can be paralyzing. Your shock and confusion are overwhelming.

(5) **Learned Helplessness:** There may be genuine passivity and a sense of overwhelming hopelessness that there is nothing you can do to alter your predicament. Although this may fluctuate with strategies of resistance you employ, acceptance and resignation set in.

(6) **Love & Hope:** You may genuinely believe the myth that love conquers all and do not want to give up on your marriage. You hold on to his promises to change during the honeymoon stage.

23 REASONS TO "STAY"

(7) **Investment:** You carefully weigh everything you have invested into building your relationship: your time, energy, love, and dedication. It is natural to not want to give up on that after many years of building a life and a marriage together.

(8) **Illusion:** You may believe in the illusion of a real relationship with your spouse since you share a home and property, have acquired many material possessions and attachments, and have children you are raising jointly.

(9) **Traditionalist:** Whether you are a fox or a hare, you feel bound by the contract of marriage, committed to preserving the family unit, and do not consider divorce a valid option.

(10) **Commitment to Children:** It is natural for any mother to worry about how her kids will be affected adversely by the separation, seek to avoid breaking up the family unit, and feel pressure from herself/family/society to fit the traditional family model.

(11) **Success Oriented:** Convinced you must try harder at saving your marriage, your entire focus is on being successful as you place the onus on yourself to achieve this.

(12) **Reputation:** Influenced by society, you may strive to protect your own reputation and that of your spouse. In a desire to save face you may maintain your silence. You may anticipate rejection, fear others will disbelieve you, or be consumed by shame and embarrassment. If your partner spread rumors to ruin your reputation and destroy your credibility, you may be humiliated.

23 REASONS TO "STAY"

(13) *Support:* When others discover the truth, you fear losing ties to family, friends, community, and culture. You loyalty to tradition might be questioned. You fear coming forth could aggravate your situation further or lead to bein abandoned by those you love the most.

(14) *Finances:* The harsh reality of separation may worry you about your change in socioeconomic status and th financial loss you might suffer.

(15) *Limited Options:* Even if you wish to leave, you may have no place to go without a support system, unable t find low-cost housing, or feel too ashamed to ask family or friends.

(16) *Independence:* If you have been co-dependent or married for some time, the fear of being on your own can b intimidating and overwhelming.

(17) *Being Alone:* Even if abuse is not an issue, separation or the ending of a marriage brings up many fears that a quite natural.

(18) *Immigration:* If you are an immigrant, there may be language barriers and visa issues that increase your feelin of total dependence on your spouse.

THE POWER TO BREAK FREE WORKBOOK   37

23 REASONS TO "STAY"

(19) **Minorities:** You may be confounded by additional obstacles if you belong to minority racial groups or whether you are a bisexual, alcoholic, disabled, or elderly.

(20) **Legal Constraints:** With limited financial resources and possibly no money of your own, you may not be able to afford legal representation.

(21) **His Manipulation:** You might also succumb to the sweetness your partner displays as he tries to win you over during the honeymoon phase.

(22) **Second Chance:** You might believe in giving your partner another chance listening to clichés such as: *"It takes two. Love conquers all. You can rise above it. Be glad you have a roof over your head. Take it with a grain of salt. Keep trying. Never give up. You can't expect too much. People don't always mean what they say. Keep smiling. He doesn't know any better. It's just a phase. Accept others the way they are. You create your own reality. Nobody said life was easy. For better or worse."*[30]

(23) **Closure:** Unresolved feelings may drive your desire for an apology. You still long to hear your partner admit to the abuse and confess how deeply he has hurt you.

DECIDING TO STAY OR LEAVE

If you are still in an abusive relationship, be honest with yourself as you answer these questions. Checkmark those that apply to you and write your answer below.

Evaluating yourself: Excerpts adapted from *Why Does He Do That?*[31]

❑ Do you have a sense of joy in your life?

❑ Is your energy and motivation declining, or do you feel depressed?

❑ Is your self-opinion and self-worth declining?

❑ Have you distanced yourself from friends or family because he makes those relationships difficult?

❑ Are you afraid of him?

❑ Are you constantly preoccupied with the relationship and how to fix it?

❑ Do you feel like you can't do anything right? Are you always trying to prove yourself? Do the problems in the relationship always seem like your fault?

❑ Do you walk away from an argument with confusion?

Evaluating your spouse: Excerpts adapted from *The Verbally Abusive Relationship.*[32]

❑ Does he have a sense of joy in his life?

❑ Does he speak openly and honestly about himself?

❑ Is his humor often at the expense of others, or is it bitter or intimidating, or does it make you uncomfortable?

❑ Does he seem distrustful of others? Is his world composed of "good guys" and "bad guys?"

❑ Does he always seem angry and conflicted and use you as a scapegoat for venting his emotions?

DECIDING TO STAY OR LEAVE

Evaluating your interaction: Excerpts adapted from *The Verbally Abusive Relationship.*[33]

❑ Does he enrich your life and bring you joy?

❑ Do you feel a genuine connection and rapport with him?

❑ Do you think in the same way and share the same dreams?

❑ Does he show goodwill towards you and others?

❑ Is there a best-friend quality to your relationship?

❑ Do you feel relaxed with him? Do you laugh together?

❑ Do you feel warmth and understanding from him?

❑ Can you be yourself around him without criticism?

❑ Does he express interest in your thoughts, ideas, feelings, opinions, plans, experiences?

❑ Is time spent with him not as pleasant as you usually anticipate?

❑ Does he seem to understand or remember things differently from you?

❑ How do you make decisions about how to use your leisure time? How do you handle separate time, separate friends, and separate interests? Do you have privacy?[34]

❑ Are you allowed to disagree without feeling wounded or angry?[35]

DECIDING TO STAY OR LEAVE

Evaluating Abuse:

❑ How has the abuse affected your quality of life?

❑ What are the different ways he tries to control you?

❑ How often do abusive incidents occur?

❑ Does the abuse continue to escalate in severity or frequency despite your efforts?

❑ Are you compromising on the safety of your children?

❑ How does he make you feel threatened or unsafe?

Following excerpts from *Why is it Always About You? Saving Yourself from the Narcissists in Your Life.*[36]

❑ What buttons of yours does he push?

❑ What do your feelings tell you to do? Do you act on these urges?

❑ What have you tried in the past? What has not worked?

❑ Are there others who can help you?

❑ Consider the costs of remaining with him. What are you giving up? What are you getting in exchange?

❑ Is it worth it to continue to stay in the relationship?

❑ How has the abuse changed you? How has it impacted your relationships, ability to function, parenting skills, etc.?

THE POWER TO BREAK FREE WORKBOOK 41

EVALUATING CHANGE

Benefits of Abusive Behavior: Adapted from *Why Does He Do That?*[37]
- ❏ Intrinsic satisfaction of power and control
- ❏ Getting his way
- ❏ Someone on whom to take out his problems
- ❏ Free labor from you while he enjoys leisure and freedom
- ❏ Being center of attention with priority given to his needs and satisfying his ego
- ❏ Financial control
- ❏ Ensuring his career, education, and goals are prioritized
- ❏ Public status of partner/father without the sacrifices
- ❏ Approval of friends and relatives
- ❏ Ability to enforce double standards

Possibility of Change:
- ❏ Is there any evidence he will change?
- ❏ If you ask him to examine his behavior, can he admit to his violence? Can he see how it has hurt you?
- ❏ Is he genuinely motivated to change? Why do you believe so?
- ❏ Is he willing to let you hold him accountable for his behaviors?
- ❏ Does he show a true sense of remorse? Has he worked to make amends for his behavior?
- ❏ Is he willing to do therapy, join a batterers intervention group, or take any other steps you feel are necessary?
- ❏ How effective have you been at changing the relationship so far?
- ❏ What, if anything, is different in your relationship now?
- ❏ Has the power dynamic between you changed in any way?

Checklist for Sincerity:
- ❏ Recognize his abusive behavior, admit his choice to use violence instead of another alternative, and see how his actions hurt you.
- ❏ Genuinely feel remorse, seek ways to make amends, build your trust, and ensure he will never be violent again.
- ❏ Stop blaming you and accept full responsibility for his actions and their consequences.
- ❏ Seek necessary help without you having to ask him.
- ❏ Be patient if you are angry and allow you full freedom to express your rage towards him.
- ❏ Deal with the abusiveness itself instead of all the excuses he makes.
- ❏ Be willing to let go of his need for power and dominance and having control over you.
- ❏ Learn to have respect for you as well as for all women.
- ❏ Willingness to listen to you, allow you to express yourself, and develop true empathy.
- ❏ Be truly motivated to be a better person and treat you well consistently.
- ❏ Actively seek personal change himself and not just because you, the community, or the legal system insist he do so.
- ❏ Be committed to therapy for the long haul and demonstrate how he has changed.
- ❏ He must willingly face himself, his insecurities, denial, fear, and his past.
- ❏ Accept that overcoming abusiveness is likely to be a lifelong process.[38]

List all the ways you would like him to change.

What would you like him to apologize for?

EXERCISES TO PROCESS ABUSE

The following exercises to process your abuse more effectively will develop your clarity and self-awareness, build strength, and increase confidence in your ability to heal and break free. Take your time with each one of these empowering exercises.

1.   Make a list of pro's and con's for your abuser. Do the same to evaluate your relationship. Next to all the pro's see how fleeting and deceptive these traits may be.

PRO'S   *CON'S*

2.   Analyze and process his abusive behavior. How did he isolate you? How did he threaten you?

EXERCISES TO PROCESS ABUSE

3. List the verbally abusive comments he made or hurtful names he has called you. See how each one was a lie designed to crush your spirits. Write something positive about yourself instead to replace each insult.

4. Write down your spouse's unrealistic demands and expectations of you as a wife, mother, housekeeper, daughter-in-law, etc. See the double standard he uses to enforce this.

5. Make a list of all the sacrifices and compromises you made throughout the relationship. See how each one contributed to surrendering your voice and your power. Write down ways to reclaim your voice and your power.

EXERCISES TO PROCESS ABUSE

6. Examine how you let your abuser define who you are and how you slowly but surely lost your identity to him. Write down ways to reclaim your identity.

7. List how you feel dependent on him emotionally, financially, socially, etc. Write down ways to become more independent by taking small or big steps. Make a list of resources and people you can count on for help.

8. When you feel ready, list the most difficult parts of the abuse that are challenging to talk about. What flashbacks continue to resurface?

EXERCISES TO PROCESS ABUSE

9. Remember a time when you felt happy, at peace, safe. How is it distinctive from what you feel now? Have close family or friends list what is different about you, what has changed since the marriage, and what seems different after separation.

10. Somatic trauma resolution exercise: Allow yourself to mentally replay the abusive incident. Remember where you were, all the details of the setting, and then what he did, what he said, the look in his eyes. Conjure up your memories-how you felt, how you reacted, the physical sensations in your body of fear or anxiety. Now, rewrite the scene so you stand up to your abuser, say no, and feel your strength. Track the sensations you feel physically as you reclaim your personal power. Do this with as many abusive memories as you need to heal the trauma.

11. How did the idea of having a successful marriage motivate you and fuel your actions? Do you still blame yourself for the "failure" of your marriage? It is critical to recognize you are not to blame. List the ways in which *he* failed you.

SAFETY PLANNING

An advocate at a women's shelter will assist you in creating an individualized plan to keep you and your children safe when you decide to leave. A safety plan will minimize your risk level by creating a safety network and securing your home. Take any extra precautionary measures that are necessary. Checkmark specific steps you have been made aware of or already taken to protect yourself. [39]

- ☐ Avoid rooms without exits to have arguments
- ☐ Avoid the kitchen where knives can be used as weapons
- ☐ Change door locks, passcodes, and phone numbers
- ☐ Add a security system
- ☐ Be prepared with a list of contact numbers and a neighbor to call in an emergency
- ☐ Know how to contact a local women's shelter or agency
- ☐ Use a code word to alert family or friends to call the police if necessary
- ☐ Avoid staying home alone
- ☐ Vary routines and route to work
- ☐ Screen phone calls, save any messages he leaves to use as evidence
- ☐ Notify children's school or colleagues at work of pressing situation
- ☐ If meeting assailant, only do so in public places where there are witnesses
- ☐ Determine escape plan if there is an emergency
- ☐ Plan how to stay safe and secure at a new location

Pack an emergency bag with essentials to get away. Include the following:
- ☐ Cash, credit cards, ATM cards, checkbook
- ☐ House and car keys
- ☐ Address book of contact numbers
- ☐ Copy of all prescriptions and month's supply of medications

Copies of important documents:
- ☐ ID cards, driver's license, passports, green card or immigration papers
- ☐ Social security card, health insurance card
- ☐ Birth certificate, marriage certificate, divorce papers
- ☐ Restraining orders, custody orders, children's school records
- ☐ Bank account numbers
- ☐ Car title, registration, and insurance information

Do you feel safe now? What measures have you taken to ensure your safety after separation? What other extra measures can you take now?

RESOURCES FOR VICTIMS

Be sure to take advantage of resources in your community such as your local domestic violence center. Checkmark resources you have already accessed or those you think you will benefit from.

- ❐ Stay at a safe-house if your security is threatened in your home where you can receive crisis intervention counseling and be in a supportive environment with other women.
- ❐ Call the National Domestic Violence Hotline at 1-800-799-SAFE, a wonderful 24 hour resource and receive advice and coaching from trained personnel during a crisis. There are also hotlines for specific ethnicities who do not speak English.
- ❐ A local domestic violence shelter may have a donation center where you can obtain immediate necessities such as food and clothing for yourself and your children.
- ❐ Confide in family and friends you trust and who will be supportive.
- ❐ Speak to a therapist you connect with and who can provide clarity to see the pattern of abuse you have been trapped in.
- ❐ Attend regular weekly support groups.
- ❐ Speak with other survivors who can offer encouragement, support, and guidance.
- ❐ Local agencies should be able to effectively navigate resources and services for you and network with housing groups, legal resources, local law enforcement, and minority/religious communities.
- ❐ Find an advocate who can direct you to resources at various stages in your healing process and guide you towards appropriate intervention strategies.
- ❐ Visit a library and research domestic violence books that will empower you with knowledge.
- ❐ Look for films and documentaries on domestic violence at the library that might be helpful to realize you are not alone.
- ❐ Local centers may also have legal advocates and free legal counsel to aid with restraining orders, divorce proceedings, custody issues, or immigration concerns.
- ❐ Look for local job and career training, resume building assistance, and English language training to provide the tools you need to be independent.
- ❐ Low-cost housing options may be available in your area.
- ❐ Sign up for self-defense classes with a trainer to build your confidence.
- ❐ Find a physical trainer who can facilitate getting in touch with your physical body again and overcome your tendency to disassociate and neglect yourself.
- ❐ Join a local yoga studio and attend yoga or meditation classes for stress reduction.
- ❐ Visit a spa and treat yourself to a relaxing massage or soothing beauty treatment.
- ❐ Visit an acupuncture clinic where a trained acupuncturist can address your PTSD symptoms.

What other resources in your community can you take advantage of?

What resources do you wish were available that are not provided on the list?

ASKING FOR SUPPORT

Many may want to support you and not know how. Do not be afraid to articulate your needs. Here are numerous ways you can ask for support.

1. Don't blame me.
2. Help me in whatever way *I* think is best. Trust I am the expert of my own life.
3. Be empathic. Validate my pain and suffering. See my point of view. Believe me.
4. Take time to listen to me and hear my story when I feel comfortable enough to share it with you.
5. If I am not yet ready to break my silence, I need to know you are there for me whenever I do decide to open up.
6. Don't be afraid to reach out and let me know you are here to help. Just calling to "check in" once in awhile shows me you are concerned.
7. Be gentle. Any advice or criticism that is harsh or controlling, or dictates what I should or should not do reminds me of my abusive partner.
8. Be aware that I am sensitive to conflict.
9. Be patient with me and acknowledge I need time to heal, find clarity, and sort through my confusion and pain.
10. Encourage me to feel confident and know I have the ability to make wise decisions for myself.
11. Recognize when I take a step to protect myself.
12. Respect and protect my right for confidentiality and build my trust.
13. Be persistent in letting me feel your support even if you doubt your ability to help.
14. Do not pressure me to leave my spouse. It must be my decision alone. I need to know you will be there for me whatever I decide and whenever I choose to leave him.
15. Do not denigrate or attack my partner because I have been conditioned to be defensive of him.
16. Focus on strategies to prioritize my safety. Express your concerns if you fear for my safety.
17. Help me appreciate my own strengths.
18. Listen to my fears about being a single parent and do not dismiss them.
19. Help me rebuild my life again and listen to how I want to be supported. I might not have the answers right away and might need time to figure this out for myself.

Who might you ask for support that you have not approached yet?

List any additional ways others can support you:

WAYS TO INTERVENE WITH CHILDREN

For mothers, there are numerous challenges to help children recover from being raised in an abusive household. The following strategies for intervention are from *Not to People Like Us*.[40] Checkmark which methods you have already been proactive about and which ones you would like to incorporate. List your challenges with some of these methods below.

❐   Explain the situation in language children can understand.

❐   Tell them the violence is not their fault.

❐   Give them permission to talk about the violence.

❐   Help make a safety plan they can follow.

❐   Find someone outside the family with whom they can share their feelings.

❐   Let them know others have had similar experiences.

❐   Discuss the situation with domestic violence or protective services staff to find out how else you can help the children.

MYTHS ABOUT COMMUNITY INVOLVEMENT

It is imperative to dismantle the following misperceptions regarding community involvement that prevent true comprehension of the dynamics surrounding domestic violence. Checkmark any myths that people in your life have believed.

- ❑ Women are not affected by cultural stereotypes and beliefs about relationship abuse.
- ❑ Abuse is restricted to certain communities such as lower socio-economic levels, certain ethnic groups, or specific strata of society.
- ❑ Turning to religious or community leaders for assistance will always prove useful. They will readily support you to make the right decisions for your safety.
- ❑ Anyone you confide in or seek help from, including friends and family, will support you unconditionally and not turn their back on you.
- ❑ Those who support you will be understanding, not question your decisions or motivations, and will always approve of leaving your spouse.
- ❑ Health care personnel will easily recognize if you are a victim of domestic violence and take necessary action.
- ❑ The legal system, police and law enforcement, and health care personnel are sensitive to victims' issues.
- ❑ When police are involved, they will always protect a victim.
- ❑ If community members are aware of abusive altercations, they will intervene promptly, choose to be involved, and call for help or assistance.
- ❑ When you reveal the abuse to family members, they will support you without fail, encouraging and prompting you to leave an abusive spouse.
- ❑ If family members witness abuse, they will intervene immediately and stop the abusive behavior.
- ❑ Those who are more familiar with legal resources will readily seek the help of law enforcement and not hesitate to obtain a restraining order.
- ❑ All victims will readily seek help from a mental health counselor given the opportunity and not believe there is any stigma attached to therapy.
- ❑ All victims will readily seek medical help if they are injured.

Which of these myths infuriates you the most? Why?

COMMUNITY'S LACK OF SUPPORT

It may have taken you years to overcome your silence and secrecy to finally reach out for help. When you did so, you may have been shocked by the reactions you received from the community. Society often perpetuates abuse through:

(1) Misperceptions, myths, and stereotypes
(2) Adherence to traditional gender roles
(3) Stigma attached to abuse or divorce
(4) Lack of support for victim

Checkmark any of the following reactions you experienced when others did not support you and why it hurt you.

❑ Sense of disbelief

❑ Shun or blame you

❑ Lack of action

❑ Neutral stand or silence

❑ Misguided coaching

❑ Enabling abuser

7 LEVELS OF COMMUNITY REACTIONS

Betrayals: Who did you feel betrayed by and why? Which betrayal has been the hardest to accept?

❐   *Level 1* Friends & family

❐   *Level 2* Neighbors & coworkers

❐   *Level 3* Religious/spiritual leaders & associations

❐   *Level 4* Therapists & social workers

❐   *Level 5* Medical personnel & caregivers

❐   *Level 6* Law enforcement & legal representatives

❐   *Level 7* Social service organizations

COMMUNITY'S 5 STAGES OF ACCEPTANCE

Most people will go through these 5 stages of acceptance after hearing your confession of victimization before they can fully support you.

(1) **Shock:** Experience shock, denial, and disbelief.
(2) **Process:** Need time to process and integrate information.
(3) **Guilt:** Blame themselves for not seeing the signs sooner or taking action.
(4) **Acceptance:** Recognition that this is the reality of the situation.
(5) **Action:** Be ready for a call to action and ways to support a victim.

As you have watched the reactions of those you confide in, how do you respond to their shock? Do you wish you had confided in them earlier?

As they process this information, how does this make you feel?

When they feel guilt or blame themselves for not taking action, how do you respond to this?

When they finally come to terms with and accept your confession, how do you respond? Do you blame them for taking this long to accept the reality of abuse?

When those you confide in are ready to take action, what is it that you would most like their help with? Do you articulate this to them?

Are you clear on how society can be supportive of your needs?

Do you ask them to take a strong stand against violence and perpetrators?

What do you think is the best way to create a solid network and infrastructure to support an abuse-free community?

5 STAGES OF HEALING: Stage 1 Recognition

Every victim journeys through 5 distinct stages of healing. Describe your recognition at each of these levels.

(a) Understanding you are a victim

(b) Identifying *how* you have been victimized

(c) Comprehending your partner's true nature

(d) Ascertaining whether change is genuine or an illusion

(e) Grasping how you may have co-created this reality or perpetuated the abusive dynamic by staying

5 STAGES OF HEALING: Stages 2-4

Stage 2 Breaking your silence How have you chosen to do so?

Stage 3 Stop the cycle of violence What steps did you take?

Stage 4 Reclaim your power

(a) How did you set limits, establish boundaries, & demand change?

(b) How did you assert your rights?

(c) Personal power: What has made you feel powerful?

STAGE 5 OPEN TO THE HEALING PROCESS

For each of these aspects of the healing process, answer the questions below. Come back to these questions periodically (in a month, six months, a year) and see how your answers may have changed.

(a) Face heartbreak: *What has been the most difficult thing to accept or let go of?*

(b) Accept & process victimization: *What has been the most difficult part of accepting this reality?*

(c) Cope with layers of emotion, trauma, & wounding: *What is your deepest wounding?*

(d) Practice forgiveness: *Are you willing to forgive yourself?*

(e) Embrace transformation & empowerment: *How do you wish to transform yourself? List ways you feel empowered.*

FORGIVENESS

You might feel pressure from others to forgive your spouse, but you are the only who can determine if you choose to do so and when you are emotionally ready. Deciding whether it is appropriate to forgive your partner or not should be determined by three conditions described in *It's My Life Now*:[41]

(1) Are his acts forgivable?

(2) Will it help you heal to forgive him?

(3) Are you ready to forgive?

The most critical aspect of your healing is to forgive yourself. List your reasons for forgiving yourself.

Only if you feel ready to do so, make a list of others you wish to forgive and why you choose to do so.

CLOSURE

Even if you are not yet ready to forgive your partner, you may feel the need for closure to address unresolved aspects of your relationship. Write a goodbye letter to your partner and pour out your heart whether you choose to send it to him or not. Do not be afraid to express everything you have held back.

KEY GOALS OF THERAPY

It may be challenging to find the right therapist to confide in. Checkmark the following goals of therapy that your therapist is following. If he/she is not, find someone who can be cognizant of these goals and make you feel comfortable.

- ☐ They acknowledge your initial visit might be the first time you are breaking your silence and understand what a monumental step you have taken coming forth.
- ☐ Offer you an objective perspective on your abusive situation.
- ☐ Help you "recognize that the abuse you have endured is inappropriate, unacceptable, and criminal."[42]
- ☐ Empower you by focusing on your acceptance and choices that trapped you instead of harping on your spouse's mistreatment and bad behavior.
- ☐ Gently show your participation in co-creating the reality of abuse without blaming you or making you feel worse about yourself.
- ☐ Does not dictate the speed through which you must work through your issues. Respects your healing process on your timetable.
- ☐ After the abuser's repetitive denial of your experience, aids in facilitating the process to trust yourself again, believe in your perceptions, and listen to your instincts.
- ☐ Recognize what stage you are at so your therapy is stage specific. In the earlier stage, you may seek therapy to learn better coping skills, techniques to impede the batterer's behavior, and enhance your resolution to save your marriage. Leaving your spouse may not be an idea you want to entertain yet. Emphasize safety and building your strength and clarity to change your behavior patterns.
- ☐ In later stages, encourages you to gain independent skills to break free. Treats you as the expert of your experience and guides you on your path of self-awareness, building confidence, and feeling empowered to move past the trauma.
- ☐ Asks you for proof if you insist on preserving the marriage. This may force you to examine your situation more objectively without blind hope or unhealthy attachment.
- ☐ Builds your strength, confidence, hope, awareness, and anything else that has been destroyed by your abuser. "The skilled therapist hooks onto that tiny glimmer of the positive and uses it in the healing process."[43]

Do you feel confident your therapist is helping you meet all these key goals of therapy? Why do you believe so?

LIST OF HEALING MODALITIES

There are a plethora of healing modalities that address all levels of body, mind, and spirit. Incorporating these powerful tools facilitates integration into wholeness. Checkmark any that you have already tried and how it benefited you. Checkmark which therapies you are interested in trying and why you think it might benefit you.

❑ **Acupuncture** is an excellent way to deal with trauma and symptoms of PTSD, reduce stress and anxiety, enhance energy, process various emotions, balance hormones, improve sleep, and boost immunity. This subtle energy work will assist in finding clarity and strength and powerfully facilitate inner transformation. Visit www.nccaom.org to find a local acupuncturist.

❑ **Somatic Trauma Resolution (STR)** is a technique developed to track sensations in the physical body to release unconscious trauma patterns that have become embedded in the psyche. Becoming aware of bodily sensations that might have been triggered during the traumatic incident itself and using those same sensations to rewire the nervous system heals the trauma. To find a practitioner, visit www.traumahealing.com.

❑ **Cranio-sacral therapy** is a potent technique designed to balance the central nervous system, release restrictions in the cranio-sacral system, and enhance physiology, by using gentle touch to stimulate the flow of cerebrospinal fluid. It is a powerful way to relax body and mind. To find a practitioner, visit www.upledger.com.

❑ **Massage** or any type of bodywork is grounding and centering. After the numbness and disassociation a victim experiences, it is necessary to connect with the physical body again and be able to deeply relax. Your spouse may never have touched you in a comforting, loving way or with kindness and it is important to be able to experience this. To find a massage therapist, visit www.ncbtmb.org.

❑ **Yoga** provides deep stretching, physical conditioning, and body awareness. The mental and emotional benefits of yoga are profound and increase energy, improve sleep, and reduce stress and anxiety. To find a teacher, visit www.yogaalliance.org or www.bksiyengar.com. In particular, restorative yoga uses the breath in certain poses held with supportive props to induce deep relaxation. To find a restorative yoga teacher, visit www.restorativeyogateachers.com.

❑ **Meditation**, a branch of yoga, involves training yourself to deeply relax at will. Breathing techniques and stress management exercises are centering and teach detachment from pain and suffering as you discover your core of bliss. Developing self-awareness and cultivating inner peace is invaluable.

❑ **Ayurveda** is an ancient, holistic medical system of India that integrates understanding one's body type with dietary remedies, synchronizing one's lifestyle with natural rhythms, using herbal medications to balance mind and body, detoxification techniques to cleanse on every level, and bodywork such as marma therapy (acupressure). To find a practitioner, visit www.ayurvedicpractitioner.com.

LIST OF HEALING MODALITIES

☐ **Panchakarma** is a vigorous, detoxification technique used in Ayurveda that is a minimum of seven days long. It includes mono-diet fasting, herbal teas and remedies, yoga and meditation, daily massage with medicated herbal oils, herbal steam, skincare remedies, *shirodhara* (technique to calm the nervous system), and a number of other procedures customized to the individual and designed to achieve balance of body, mind, and spirit. To schedule treatment at a renowned center, visit www.Ayurveda.com.

☐ **Herbal therapy** uses various herbs to calm the mind, target the nervous system, resolve symptoms of trauma and stress, and restore balance on the cellular level. Only seek the advice of a well-qualified herbalist and do not attempt to self-medicate.

☐ **Aromatherapy** uses therapeutic essential oils that target different systems of the body and are deeply relaxing, grounding, and balancing for various emotions.

☐ **Martial Arts** involves learning self-defense techniques, cultivating discipline, building strength, and is empowering. Slow moving, graceful forms like tai chi create a sense of peace and stillness within.

What other therapies or techniques have you tried? Write about your experience here. What has been the most helpful way for you to get back in balance? What would you recommend to other victims and why?

EMBRACING YOUR FUTURE

The following exercises are designed to embrace your future and look forward to creating a new abuse-free life. Take time to deeply contemplate your answers to each of these questions.

(1) Create positive interpretations of lessons learned from your marriage and how they can liberate you.

(2) Envision an abuse-free life and where you think you will be in a month, six months, a year, or five years down the road.

(3) How will you step outside of your comfort zone and take risks to build your courage and self-confidence? What is one action you can commit to this week?

EMBRACING YOUR FUTURE

(4) Create a mission statement for your new life and for dealing with your separation/ divorce to empower you.

(5) Many victims hold onto the marriage because of the contract they feel they have made with their spouse, his family, church, or as a way of upholding cultural values, quoting "in sickness and health, until death do us part." Make a new contract with yourself, a list of promises to put yourself, your health, and your safety first.[44]

(6) Positive visualization is a powerful technique to shift your perspective and transition out of old behavior patterns. Imagine an abuse-free life where you are nurtured, living in a peaceful home, surrounded by friends and family who support you. Envision following your dreams, pursuing your interests, and not being held back. Describe what this scenario would look like.

QUALITIES YOU SEEK IN A NEW PARTNER

Make your wish list of all the qualities you seek in a new partner for when you are ready to embrace a new relationship. Do not hold back from creating your dream man. Then prioritize these qualities in order of importance to you. When you start a new relationship, evaluate how many of these qualities he possesses to determine if you are compromising on qualities that are really important to you. If so, reassess your relationship.

AFFIRMATIONS

Repeating daily affirmations starts to shift the energy of your nervous system from that of a victim to a woman who possesses power and assuredness. Choose one or more of these statements that resonate deeply with you. It will prove cathartic. Commit to a specific time each day to recite these. Looking at yourself in the mirror may be helpful.

1) I have the power to break free.
2) I am strong. I am beautiful. I am healthy. I am confident.
3) I am intelligent. I am wise.
4) I respect myself. I am true to myself. I honor myself.
5) I am safe. I am protected.
6) I will rest and heal my wounds. I will recover.
7) I will nurture and take care of myself. I will be compassionate towards myself.
8) I am not to blame for what happened. I forgive myself.
9) I don't have to compromise. I deserve better.
10) I have the ability to make my own decisions and decide what is best for me.
11) I trust myself. I will listen to my instincts and my inner voice.
12) I am independent. I can make my own choices and decisions.
13) Only I can define my own life. Nobody else can define who I am.
14) I trust my inner voice, intuition, feelings, and perception.
15) My life is valuable. I cherish my life.
16) I deserve freedom and respect.
17) I have a strong, powerful voice.
18) I have integrity and truth on my side.
19) I am free. I am untouchable. I am powerful.
20) I have unlimited potential and unlimited power within me. I can do anything.
21) I will be creative and resourceful as I open into my healing process.
22) I feel positive.
23) I will have a happier, healthier life.
24) I embrace my future with open arms.
25) I love who I am. I love who I will be.
26) I am hopeful, determined, courageous, inspired.
27) I am passionate about life.
28) I will be transformed through this experience.
29) I am open to my possibilities for the future. I can do anything.
30) I am at peace with myself. I am at peace with the world.

Write your own personal affirmations here. What do you want to shift in your own life? What do you want more of?

STRATEGIES FOR SELF-CARE

Taking time for yourself, your healing, and finding your way again is crucial. Investing energy and time into self-care will pay off. Here are a number of suggestions to do so. Choose one way to nurture yourself daily:

- ❐ Create a space for yourself every day to do something relaxing and nurturing, have a personal spiritual practice, and consciously work on emotional cleansing. Nourish yourself spiritually.
- ❐ Stay connected to what you find meaningful and what brings you joy. Do what inspires you. Be creative; there are no rules to healing.
- ❐ Try to have fun, make new friends, participate in enjoyable activities, and begin a new phase of your life.
- ❐ Purify your environment and light candles, burn incense, and reclaim your personal space.
- ❐ Observe your diet and choose healthy, delicious foods to nurture your body and focus on self-care after so much neglect.
- ❐ Exercise, develop an intense fitness regime, or hire a personal trainer to get in optimal physical shape.
- ❐ Write in a journal, pour out your heart, say everything you never had a chance to say to your partner.
- ❐ Spend time outdoors in the beauty of nature, whether it is sitting by the ocean, walking through the forest, or simply strolling in your backyard.
- ❐ Let yourself heal and rejuvenate.
- ❐ Set new goals for your career path or finding a new direction in your life again.
- ❐ Spend extra quality time with your children and embark on a new adventure.
- ❐ Travel to a new, exotic destination.

Make a list of your personal goals for self care:

From where do you draw strength and inspiration? How can you embrace that more in your life?

ENDING ABUSE GLOBALLY

We must all play our part in ending abuse globally. Now that you have the firsthand experience and insight, what steps can you take to be involved? When does it feel right for you to participate in this global movement?

Here are **7 immediate actions** we can take towards this cause. Checkmark which ones you can commit to now or below each write when in the future it is realistic for you to do so.

☐ Support your local women's shelters by donating household supplies, clothing, or anything else they might find useful. Call them directly to ask what they need. Many agencies will have "wish lists" for their clients.

☐ Donate funds to women's resources and centers that are in dire need of adequate funding. Many donations are tax-deductible.

☐ "Adopt" a victim by asking your local shelter if they have this program. Your donations will go specifically to her immediate financial requirements whether it is legal bills, housing, or childcare.

☐ Volunteer time at local women's agencies to help with understaffing and the overwhelming response these centers have to adequately address victim's needs. Many centers can see approximately 1,000 new victims every month if not more.

☐ Inform and educate your religious institutions about partnering with domestic violence agencies, when to refer to them, and how to support women.

☐ Speak to your children's teachers at school about increasing education and awareness about domestic violence in every grade level and engage them in meaningful discussion as to preventing this crime.

☐ Discuss gender violence openly without deeming it taboo. Remove the shame and stigma so women are not afraid to break their silence.

JOURNAL FOR SELF-REFLECTION

Writing is an effective way to process your emotions, uncover what is in your heart, and not be afraid to express yourself in the privacy of your journal. Use the following section to write longer answers to any of the questions from the previous sections if you desire to. There is an inspirational quote at the beginning of each page. Feel free to write why that quote speaks to you. Answer the questions below to reflect on your experience using this workbook.

Have the exercises in this book brought you more clarity about your relationship?

Have you found the tools that you need to heal?

Are you more honest with yourself? Do you pay attention to your instincts more?

What other changes have you noticed as you become more self-aware and stronger day by day?

If you were offering advice to another victim, what would you say to inspire her?

Who has been your best supporter during this process? What could you do for them to acknowledge their support?

What are your hesitations or fears about going public about your victimization?

After allowing sufficient time to prioritize your own healing, how would you give back to the community? What could you do to help other victims on their journey?

Freedom and love go together. Jiddu Krishnamurti

The world breaks everyone and afterward many are strong at the broken places. Ernest Hemingway

No one saves us but ourselves. No one can and no one may. We ourselves must walk the path. Buddha

Freedom is never voluntarily given by the oppressor; it must be demanded by the oppressed. –Martin Luther King Jr.

Too often we underestimate the power of a touch, a smile, a kind word, a listening ear, an honest compliment, or the smallest act of caring, all of which have the potential to turn a life around. Leo Buscaglia

You have within you the strength, the patience, and the passion to reach for the stars and change the world. Harriet Tubman

A journey of a thousand miles must begin with a single step.   Lao Tzu

And the day came when the risk to remain tight in a bud was more painful than the risk it took to blossom. Anais Nin

True love is when your heart and your mind are saying the same thing.   Leanna L. Bartra

What matters is how well we have loved.   President Barack Obama

The only journey is the one within.   Rainer Maria Rilke

In the midst of movement and chaos, keep stillness inside of you. Deepak Chopra

Although the world is full of suffering, it is also full of the overcoming of it. Helen Keller

The important thing is to be able at any moment to sacrifice what you are for what you can become.   Charles Dubois

It is never too late to be what you might have been.   George Eliot

Our lives teach us who we are.   Salman Rushdie

Vitality shows not only in the ability to persist but in the ability to start over.   F. Scott Fitzgerald

Much of your pain is the bitter potion by which the physician within you heals your sick self.   Kahlil Gibran

ABOUT THE AUTHOR

Anisha Durve, A.P. M.S.O.M.

Anisha is an acupuncture physician, ayurvedic practitioner, yoga therapist, and meditation instructor since 2000. She is a true practitioner of integrative medicine blending the wisdom of all these ancient Eastern modalities. She is an accomplished public speaker and teaches workshops and trainings for students and practitioners globally. Anisha is motivated to teach victims and survivors of gender violence integrative tools to assist in their healing journey. She has also designed workshops for acupuncturists to heal trauma from gender violence with specific treatment protocols. If you are interested in creating a holistic clinic for victims of gender violence please contact her.

She co-authored the clinical textbook "Marma Points of Ayurveda: Energy Pathways for Healing Body, Mind, and Consciousness; with a Comparison to Traditional Chinese Medicine" with her guru Dr. Vasant Lad in 2008 and published by The Ayurvedic Press. She teaches workshops on acupressure for practitioners and laypersons to learn this ancient healing art.

As a survivor of gender violence, she is committed to inspiring women who live in oppression to know that they possess the power to break free. By using a holistic visionary approach, she believes vigorous education and outreach are necessary to address the politics of abuse and oppression of women worldwide. Within the South Asian community, she aims to create a collective voice for issues specific to this subgroup. Anisha is available for speaking engagements and healing trauma workshops.

For more information please visit her personal website at www.Anisha.Guru

BIBLIOGRAPHY

Domestic Violence Resources

1. Nankani, Sandhya. *Breaking the Silence: Domestic Violence in the South Asian- American Community*. Xlibris Corporation. 2000.
2. Abraham, Margaret. *Speaking the Unspeakable: Marital Violence among South Asian Immigrants in the United States*. Rutgers University Press, New Brunswick, New Jersey. 2000.
3. Shamita Das Dasgupta. *Body Evidence: Intimate Violence Against South Asian Women in America*. Rutgers University Press, New Brunswick, New Jersey. 2007.
4. Bancroft, Lundy. *Why Does He Do That? Inside the Minds of Angry and Controlling Men*. Berkely Books: New York. 2002.
5. Weitzman, Susan, Ph.D. *Not to People Like Us: Hidden Abuse in Upscale Marriages*. Basic books: New York, 2000.
6. Gavin de Becker. *The Gift of Fear: and Other Survival Signals that Protect Us from Violence*. Dell Publishing, New York. 1997.
7. Walker, Lenore E. *The Battered Woman*. Harper & Row Publishers, New York. 1979.
8. Herman, Judith M.D. *Trauma & Recovery: The Aftermath of Violence- From Domestic Abuse to Political Terror.* Basic Books, New York, NY. 1992.
9. Jacobson, Neil and Gottmann, John. *When Men Batter Women: New Insights into Ending Abusive Relationships*. Simon & Schuster, New York. 1998.
10. Jayne, Pamela. *Ditch that Jerk: Dealing with Men who Control and Hurt Women*. Hunter House, Alameda, CA, 2000.
11. Dugan, Meg Kennedy and Hock, Roger R. *It's My Life Now: Starting Over After an Abusive Relationship or Domestic Violence*. Routledge, New York. 2006.
12. Evans, Patricia. *The Verbally Abusive Relationship: How to Recognize It and How to Respond*. Media, Avon, MA 1992.
13. Lissette, Andrea & Kraus, Richard. *Free Yourself from an Abusive Relationship: 7 Steps to Taking Back your Life*. Hunter House Publishers, Alameda, CA. 2000.
14. Betancourt, Marian. *What to Do When Love Turns Violent: A Practical Resource for Women in Abusive Relationships*. Harper Collins, New York. 1997.
15. Forward, Susan Ph.D. with Donna Frazier. *Emotional Blackmail: When the People in Your Life Use Fear, Obligation and Guilt to Manipulate You*. Harper Collins Publishers, New York, NY. 1997.

Other Resources

16. Ford, Debbie. *Spiritual Divorce- Divorce as a Catalyst for an Extraordinary Life*. Harper Collins, New York, NY. 2001.
17. Lesser, Elizabeth. *Broken Open: How Difficult Times Can Help Us Grow.* Villard Books, New York, NY. 2005.
18. Wilson, Karen Kahn. *Transformational Divorce: Discover Yourself, Reclaim your Dreams, and Embrace Life's Unlimited Possibilities*. New Harbinger Publications, Oakland, CA. 2003.
19. Hotchkiss, Sandy. *Why is it Always About You? The Seven Deadly Sins of Narcissism*. Free Press, New York, NY. 2002.
20. Wilson, James L. *Adrenal Fatigue: the Twenty-First Century Stress Syndrome*. Smart Publications, Petaluma, CA. 2001.
21. *The Merck Manual of Medical Information*. Pocket Books, New York, NY. 1997.

There are numerous valuable publications on domestic violence. The ones listed here are just a small sample.

Please visit our website at www.Power2BreakFree.com for additional online resources.

REERENCES

References

1 adapted from Evans, Patricia. *The Verbally Abusive Relationship: How Recognize It and How to Respond.* Media, Avon, MA 1992. p.118. and Lissette, Andrea & Kraus, Richard. *Free Yourself from an Abusive Relationship: 7 Steps taking Back your Life.* Hunter House Publishers, Alameda, CA 2000 p.188.

2 McGee, Susan G.S. *"20 Reasons Why She Stays: A Guide For Those WiWant to Help Battered Women."* 1995-2009. p.13.

3 *IBID* p.13.

4 Dugan, Meg Kennedy and Hock, Roger R. *It's My Life Now: Starting O After an Abusive Relationship or Domestic Violence.* Routledge, New York, 2006. p. 127.

5 Some excerpts taken from Bancroft, Lundy. *Why Does He Do That? In2 the Minds of Angry and Controlling Men.* Berkely Books: New York, 2002. p.226.

6 Family Justice Center Domestic Violence Training Notes. 2010.

7 de Becker, Gavin. *The Gift of Fear: and Other Survival Signals that Prct us from Violence.* Dell Publishing, New York, 1997. p.196.

8 *IBID* p.230.

9 Walker, Lenore E. *The Battered Woman.* Harper & Row Publishers, N\York, 1979. p.223,106,79.

10 Family Justice Center Domestic Violence Training Notes 2010.

11 Dugan, Meg Kennedy and Hock, Roger R. *It's My Life Now: Starting r After an Abusive Relationship or Domestic Violence.* Routledge, New York, 2006. p. 11.

12 Lissette, Andrea & Kraus, Richard. *Free Yourself From an Abusive R\onship: Seven Steps to Taking Back Your Life.* Hunter House Publishers, Alameda, CA 2000. p.45-46.

13 de Becker, Gavin. *The Gift of Fear: and Other Survival Signals that \ct us from Violence.* Dell Publishing, New York, 1997. p.210-212.

14 Bancroft, Lundy. *Why Does He Do That? Inside the Minds of Angry Controlling Men.* Berkely Books: New York, 2002. p.8.

15 *IBID* p.8.

16 *IBID* p.40.

17 Jayne, Pamela. *Ditch that Jerk: Dealing with Men Who Control and \ Women.* Hunter House, Alameda, CA, 2000. p.20-27.

18 de Becker, Gavin. *The Gift of Fear: and Other Survival Signals that 2ct us from Violence.* Dell Publishing, New York, 1997. p.210-212.

19 Hotchkiss, Sandy. *Why Is It Always About You? Saving Yourself Fron Narcissists in Your Life.* Free Press, New York, NY. 2002. p.72

20 Bancroft, Lundy. *Why Does He Do That? Inside the Minds of Angry Controlling Men.* Berkely Books: New York, 2002. p.152-157.

21 http://www.health.am/psy/narcissistic-personality-disorder/ Armeniædical Network. 2006 p.3.

22 Bancroft, Lundy. *Why Does He Do That? Inside the Minds of Angry Controlling Men.* Berkely Books: New York, 2002. p.91-94.

23 *IBID* p.80-83.

24 *IBID* p.96-99, 88-91, 83-85.

25 Weitzman, Susan, Ph.D. *Not to People Like Us: Hidden Abuse in Up Marriages.* Basic books: New York, 2000. p.61.

26 *The Merck Manual of Medical Information.* Pocket Books, New Yorw York, 1997. P.432-433.

27 *IBID* p.447.

28 Weitzman, Susan, Ph.D. *Not to People Like Us: Hidden Abuse in Up Marriages.* Basic books: New York, 2000. p.118.

29 Dugan, Meg Kennedy and Hock, Roger R. *It's My Life Now: Startirer After an Abusive Relationship or Domestic Violence.* Routledge, New York, 2006. p. 3, 63, 21, 193, 157, 97, 203, 85, 213.

30 Evans, Patricia. *The Verbally Abusive Relationship: How to Recognand How to Respond.* Media, Avon, MA 1992. p.110-112.

31 Bancroft, Lundy. *Why Does He Do That? Inside the Minds of Angr\Controlling Men.* Berkely Books: New York, 2002. p.130.

32 Evans, Patricia. *The Verbally Abusive Relationship: How to Recognand How to Respond.* Media, Avon, MA 1992. p.147-148.

33 *IBID* p.147-148.

34 Hotchkiss, Sandy. *Why Is It Always About You? Saving Yourself froNarcissists in your Life.* Free Press, New York, NY. 2002. p.123

35 *IBID* p.123.

36 *IBID* p.78,100,143 .

37 Bancroft, Lundy. *Why Does He Do That? Inside the Minds of AngrControlling Men.* Berkely Books: New York, 2002. p.152-157.

38 *IBID* p.341.

39 Bancroft, Lundy. *Why Does He Do That? Inside the Minds of AngiControlling Men.* Berkely Books: New York, 2002. p.228-229./ Weitzman, Susan, Ph.D. *Not to People Like Us: Hidden Abuse in Upscale Marriages.* ㅏooks: New York, 2000. p.125.

40 Weitzman, Susan, Ph.D. *Not to People Like Us: Hidden Abuse in \ Marriages.* Basic books: New York, 2000. p.173.

41 Dugan, Meg Kennedy and Hock, Roger R. *It's My Life Now: Starter After an Abusive Relationship or Domestic Violence.* Routledge, New York, 2006. p. 149.

42 *IBID* p.199.

43 *IBID* p.186.

44 Forward, Susan Ph.D. with Donna Frazier. *Emotional Blackmail: he People in Your Life Use Fear, Obligation and Guilt to Manipulate You.* Harper Collins Publishers, New York, NY, 1997. p.148.